1

Boost your **Youtube** channel

All the secrets to get subscribers and views"

INTRODUCTION

Welcome to " **Booster sa YouTube channel** ": the secrets to get subscribers and views - The ultimate guide to unlock the secrets of Youtube And reach of new heights as the creator of content. If you dream that your videos reach thousands or even millions of people, This book is for you.

AT the era of digital, Youtube To proven itself as platform where dreams become reality. That you be an amateur, an expert or A new artist, Youtube YOU offers a global platform to share your voice and your talents.

But how transform this opportunity in A enormous hit ? How cause your videos are not only watched, but also admired, shared and commented?

The key is to understand the secrets of this platform dynamic. This book is designed to provide you with

knowledge, strategies and the
advice you have
need to pass from a beginner To
A influencer Youtube.

You will learn how to create a
content convincing, To to master
photography techniques and
editing, to optimize your presence
through optimization search
engines (SEO), And Moreover.

 But this book does not stop to
teach skills techniques. He
guides you also in connection
with your audience, creating

of an engaged community and evolution continues as content creator.

THE hit on Youtube is not not a destination, but a journey exciting and constant evolution. It is a journey where lessons you learn and relationships you build are just as valuable as your views of videos.

Get ready to dive into a world of endless possibilities, exciting discoveries and exciting challenges.

That you have already started your adventure YouTube or that you are planning a trip, this book will accompany you to each stage.

As the adventure begins - get ready to boost your YouTube channel and reveal all the secrets to attracting enthusiastic subscribers and passionate views.

Chapter 1 : To understand THE Countryside of Youtube

Welcome to this journey exciting behind the scenes Youtube, there cloth digital Or

dreams are formed and where each video can become a phenomenon global.

For any content creator, new or experienced, a in-depth understanding of the ecosystem Youtube East there cornerstone of growth successful. In this chapter we we look at what makes

Youtube This that he East And let's explore concrete examples of content creators who have managed to excel in this vast universe.

Youtube transcends her Status of platform video in line. It is a vast universe where creativity, passion and authenticity are the engines.

Great travel videos to expert tutorials, vlogs analysis staff thorough, Youtube offer a endless variety of content for every taste. Inasmuch as creators, we have the opportunity to share our passion and our knowledge, make our voices heard and to inspire millions of people around the world.

An inspiring example of this magic East there chain " **Ted-Ed** ". He transforms concepts complex in animations exciting educational shed light on various topics.

That proves that Youtube can be more than just entertainment, it can be a source of learning and discovery. The success on Youtube born to limit not To publish videos and get views.

It requires keeping to aware of trends in constant evolution. Challenges viral, trending memes and trending topics can propel your content at the top of trends.

For example, the " **Bottlecap Challenge** " has inspired many creators to take up the challenge and show their skills unique.

This shows that responding to trends can be a powerful catalyst to increase the visibility. The numbers are not that part of the equation on Youtube. The commitment and community building strong are essential.

Consider the creators of content like **Casey Neistat** which interact closely with their audience. By responding to comments, by organizing Q&A sessions live and sharing personal stories, **Casey** has created a real connection with its subscribers.

The story of **Casey** We teaches that each subscriber is more than just a number, they are people who connect to your content. **PewDiePie**
: **Felix Kjellberg** , better known under the name of **PewDiePie,** is the ultimate success story of Youtube.

His video games have sparked the passionate commitment of a enormous base of fans, THE pushing

at the top with more than
100 million subscribers.

 Tasty : The **Tasty channel**
has revolutionized the way we
consume recipes
line. Their short videos and
visually appealing attracted
millions of subscribers search for
culinary inspiration.

 Casey Neistat as **Casey
Neistat** became a vlogging icon
thanks to his approach
cinematographic. His talent to tell
stories

visually appealing cultivated a loyal audience.

Emma Chamberlain : **Emma** has stormed YouTube with its fresh vlogging style and authentic. natural sound and sound honesty have created a strong bond with his generation and generated million views.

Each success is unique, but they all share a factor commmon : creativity, authenticity and dedication.

These creators understood
Youtube of bottom in fills And
used it to create
engaging experiences for their
audience. The next chapter
examines the practical steps to
create and optimize content to to
reach new heights on Youtube.

So get ready to dive in the
dynamic world of content
production, where each video
East a opportunity of shine And to
inspire.

Chapter 2 : Create A Content Captivating

Welcome to the heart of the success of YouTube: content creation attractive. In This chapter, I will guide you through the most important steps for create videos that no only attract attention, but also increase commitment and retain your audience.

We look at examples specific of creators Who have

mastered the art, revealing the strategies and techniques that led to the top.

Before of create of content, he East important to know your niche and your target audience.

Take **Binging** with **Babish** , a string that transforms the food from movies and live tv shows receipts. This particular niche has allowed the author to stand out of the sea of culinary content.

Determine This Who YOU keen And resonates with your audience potential. It will help you to focus your efforts creative.

Originality is the key to excellence. " **Vsauce** " is a extension channel scientist who shines with a original approach to subjects complex.

With of the pictures unique And of the engaging explanations, " **Vsauce** " gained subscribers because its content stood out similar videos. Don't have fear of discovering new ideas and to work on each video.

  The title and thumbnail are the first impression that you make on your potential audience. Check out the " **Click For "** **channel Taz"** Who attracted THE clicks with of the catchy titles and thumbnails expressive.

But make sure the content of the video corresponds to expectations created by the title and thumbnail. Balance curiosity and honesty is essential for earn the public's trust.

Mark Rober : the former engineer of NASA, **Mark Rober,** turns science into entertainment. His video " **Building the Perfect** Squirrel proof bird Feeder" East become viral because of its approach unique and humorous.

Liza Koshy: Liza Koshy used comedy in his videos and has created instant chemistry with His public. His energetic style and his humorous sketches have attracted millions of fans.

Linus Tech Tips : Passionate about technology, Linus Tech Tips offers reviews and honest advice. His ability to explain of the topics complex of understandably won public trust.

The king of chance : before his death tragedy, **Grant Thompson** created a string based on science experiments and adjustments. His enthusiasm contagious inspired a dedicated community.

These creators understood the importance of creating content original, high quality and engaging. Their videos are not only watched, but admired and shared. Next their example, you can explore of the outlook unique, adopt a style personal and add humor to engage your audience.

In conclusion, the creation of engaging content on YouTube requires an understanding depth of your niche, a unlimited creativity and attention to details. By combining these elements, you can not only attract attention, but also create a lasting bond with your audience. In the chapter Next, we will explore the shooting techniques and editing that will bring your creative vision.

Chapter 3: Mastering the Techniques of Shooting And of Assembly

In this chapter, we dive in the art of visual creation For Youtube. There quality of filming and editing is essential to capture audience and strengthen your online presence.

Examples of creators of performing content in these domains give us a overview of the key factors of video creation professional And engaging.

Although you don't need most expensive equipment succeed on Youtube, invest In material can considerably improve the quality of your videos.

Take the example of the creator of " **iJustine** " tech content .
The use of modern cameras enabled him to produce sharp and clear videos that have increased its credibility as as a technical expert.

However, remember that the content is king - make sure that the story you tell is the star of the video, what whatever devices you use.

Editing is where your content comes to life. Cups well-paced transitions fluids and good visual effects placed can considerably improve visual experience. " **Cinemasins** " is a channel that investigation of inconsistencies in movies.

Their thoughtful use of the quick edit to show the subtle flaws makes them both entertaining and informative. THE rhythm of your editing should match the tone and purpose of your video, keeping in mind mind attention of your audience.

Music and visual effects can set the mood and add emotion to your videos. The **Nerdwriter1 string** parses sequences of art and culture pop and fast-paced stories. A thoughtful choice of music and effects visuals improved there quality of its analysis and retains public attention. Use these elements with parsimony for avoid overloading the video, but make sure they complete your story.

Peter McKinnon : As content creator focused on photography and video, **Peter McKinnon** uses a variety equipment to create cinematic videos
impeccable. His attention to detail in filming and editing is evident in every video.

The Slow Mo Guys : This channel specializes in registration of events slow motion. Their fascinating videos are the result of using And of a creative montage of the camera, revealing details
invisible to the naked eye.

Lilly Singh: Also known as the name of "Superwoman", **Lilly Singh** adds visual effects humor to his videos. Her dynamic editing and its touch personal distinguish it from the stage of there comedy on Internet.

Casey Neistat: Casey Neistat excels once again with his distinctive editing and its narration visual. His vlogs cinematographic postponed the limits of the genre and inspired a new generation of creators.

These creators have proven that the mastery of shooting techniques of view and mounting can raise the quality of your videos to new heights. The key is to combine skills techniques with your vision creative.

By using the devices at good wisely, keeping a rhythm engaging and strengthening your message with effects, you can create content visually striking which engages and holds the attention of your audience.

In conclusion, photography and assembly are tools powerful to tell your compelling story. In the next chapter, we explore the secrets of YouTube SEO which are essential to increase the visibility of your video and attract a wider audience.

Chapter 4: Optimizing For THE SEO (SEO) on Youtube

Engine optimization search (
SEO) is stone cornerstone of an
online presence, and YouTube is
no exception. In this chapter, we
dive In THE secrets of SEO
Youtube.

real examples of creators of
content that have mastered with
success SEO us guide through
the techniques the most
important for increase the
exposure of your videos and
attract the attention of a critical
audience.

The objective of **YouTube SEO** is make your videos easy detectable by users looking for similar topics. Consider your **title,** your **description** and your **tags** like engine indicators of research.

Brian Dean 's Channel **(Backlink)** specializes in engine optimization research and its videos offer practical advice for increase your ranking in search engines.

By understanding how it works search algorithms YouTube, you can customize your content to that he either more easy To find.

THE **key words** And THE **tags** are of the elements important For THE users interested who want to find your videos. **Robert Blake** 's Channel offers growth guides online and his videos are generated based on keywords relevant.

By searching for keywords popular in your niche and naturally including them in titles, descriptions and beacons, you increase your chances of appearing in search results.

Description **is** optional extra to add **words keys** relevant And explain the content of your video. The expert YouTube " **Derral Eves** " features a step-by-step guide to optimize video metadata.

By writing descriptions clear and attractive containing precise information about the video content, you increase your credibility with search engines and viewers.

Graham Stephan : As financial content creator, **Graham Stephan** optimizes his videos to answer common questions about investment and real estate. Its **titles** and **descriptions** reflect have it aid To to hoist At pinnacle of research in its niche.

Cooking with a dog: this japanese food chain a used a pun in his title, which includes the name of a popular cartoon. This has allowed the chain to be in the lead search results from Japanese recipes.

Nathaniel Drew : during the creating videos of personal development and wellness, **Nathaniel Drew** uses targeted keywords in its descriptions to attract an audience interested in these topics. His well-optimized metadata made it possible to stand out from competitive niche market.

Brownlee Brands : **MKBHD** , a community icon technology, uses detailed descriptions and precise labels in its product review videos.
This increased his credibility as expert and earned him millions subscribers.

Discover how to optimise your videos for SEO Youtube in following these examples of creators. Do not forget that optimization is a combination of art and science - by providing quality content and using relevant keywords, you can rank high search results and engage relevant audiences in your niche.

SEO _ YouTube is an essential part of your success online. In the chapter Next, we will discuss engagement and interaction with your audience and explore how YOU can develop your community around your channel.

Chapter 5 : Engage And Interact with your Hearing

Reaching your audience is essential to create a strong and faithful community on Youtube. In This chapter, We explore ways to strengthen the commitment, encourage interaction and to build lasting relationships with your subscribers.

Concrete examples of content creators who have succeeded in creating communities involved show us important techniques for transform viewers casual in fans passionate.
 Each comment is the occasion of create A link personal with your viewers.

Take for example the thread
of product discussion
" **Unbox Therapy** ". The answers
from the authors to the comments
of the community strengthen the
sense of unity and encourage
viewers to come back for more
interaction.

Responding to comments with
honesty and care, you show that
each person is important to you.
The interactive features of
YouTube such as Stories and
surveys are tools powerful to
increase
commitment.

" **Safiya Nygaard"** uses the polls as video feeds for to take decisions community.

It creates a sense of inclusion and makes sure that community feels involved in the creative process. Don't be afraid to experiment these features to get active responses from your audience.

" **Philip DeFranco** " is the example of a creator who has made his chain a truly community. His videos commenting on the news arouse heated discussions in the comments.

By leaving room for differing opinions and encouraging debate respectful, he created a environment where viewers felt connected to each other and At Creator.

Build a community asked of time And of the efforts

constant to promote a
sense of belonging.

Shane DawsonShane **Dawson**
was able to create a community
committed by sharing personal
and honest videos.
Its viewers have
the feeling of knowing her
personally, which reinforces their
connection to her.

Jenna Marbles : by interacting
with his fans in every video and
integrating their recommendations
in its content, **Jenna Marbles** has

builds a loyal community who
feels invested in his chain.

Try it guys: this team creative
uses videos
interactive where viewers vote for
their favourites. That creates a
sense of belonging and increases
engagement.

Tana Mongeau : Tana Mongeau
his life in a raw way and
authentic that creates a link
deeply with his community.

Lively discussions and
passionate take place in the
comments of his videos. By
implementing these methods
of engagement
creators, you can create a faithful
community around your channel.

By responding to comments,
using the features
YouTube interactives and
creating space for a respectful
conversation, you create an
environment in
which your subscribers feel
valued and included.

Reaching your audience is not only a matter of numbers, it's about relationships real. In the next chapter, we will explore strategies to increase the exposure of your video via social media and cross-marketing.

Chapter 6: Using the Social Networks for Increase there Visibility

Extending your influence does not limit not To Youtube. THE media

social media and
cross-marketing can play a key
role in grow your audience and
promoting your content.

In this chapter we explore
strategies for use the media
effectively social And there
promotion cross, using concrete
examples of content creators who
have succeeded in extending their
reach
beyond of Youtube.

Social networks provide a platform to interact with your audience outside Youtube.

Take " **Hannah Hart",** which has built a fanbase on YouTube with its show of food. She also uses Instagram to share personal moments and interact with the community in a way more informal.

Use social media to show your human side and encourage your audience to interact of one manner different that on Youtube.

Every media platform social media has its own style and own audience. " **Gary Vaynerchuk** " is a social media expert and marketing that PERSONALIZE its content for each platform.

On Twitter, he share of the advice tough and engaging. On Instagram, she connects with its audience through stories authentic. By understanding the specificities of each platform, you can create content that resonates with different public.

Cross-promotion with other content creators can extend your reach exponentially. Chain " **Rhett and Link** " is known for there series " **Good legendary Morning** " and invited many designers guests To collaborate. This allowed them to present their content to a new audience and benefit from a reciprocal increase in number of subscribers.

In YOU teaming up To of the creators of content with an audience similar, you can attract the attention of new subscribers interested in your content.

David DobrikDavid Dobrik uses Instagram to share hidden moments and connect with fans authentic way. His personal stories create a close bond between him and the public.

Lilly Singh : Apart from her YouTube videos, **Lilly Singh** has a strong presence on social networks.

She shares clips of her videos, updates personal and encourages interaction with fans.

Casey Neistat as **Casey Neistat** uses Twitter to share its thoughts and interact with followers. His tweets reflect his personality and give fans insight into his daily life.

Emma **ChamberlainEmma _ Chamberlain,** the queen of vlogging, sharing moments intimate and authentic on Instagram.

He also uses Twitter to express their thoughts and create a dialogue with his followers.

By following these strategies creative, you can use the social media and marketing

crossed to extend your reach
and attract new subscribers.

The objective is to create a
coherent and attractive presence
on all platforms while respecting
the nuances of each environment.
 In conclusion, the
creation audience goes
beyond Youtube.

Social media and the
cross-marketing are tools
powerful to increase the visibility
of your content and create an
engaged community. In

the last chapter we discuss key takeaways from this book and offer you a path to becoming a creator Youtube To hit.

Chapter 7 : To plan And Consistency of Publication

Congratulations, you have undertaken an exciting journey through THE keys of hit of Youtube.

In this final chapter, we present to you a sheet of convenient route to help you succeed as a creator Youtube. We cover the main points covered in this book and illustrate them with specific examples of authors who have successfully completed these steps to achieve great peaks.

The first step to success is to find your passion and your niche. Discover 'Safiya Nygaard' who used his love fashion and beauty for create unique videos.

By identifying what you passionate, you can create a authentic and engaging content who stands out from the sea of online videos.

The quality and originality of content are important to draw attention. " **Vsauce** " was able to produce videos innovative educational engage the public. By exploring new ideas and adding your own personality, you can to offer To your viewers a memorable experience.

Engine optimization research Youtube East crucial For interested users.

" **Graham Stephan** " used relevant keywords to attract a public interested in his financial videos.

By understanding the basics of engine optimization research and using smart keywords, you can increase the visibility of your videos.

Public participation is essential for building a strong community. " **Philip DeFranco** " has created a space of lively discussion in the comments, strengthening the link with his community.

By responding to comments, using features interactive and encouraging participation, you can create an environment in which your subscribers feel valued. Social media and the cross-marketing are means efficient to expand your scope.

" **David Dobrik** " uses Instagram to show moments in backstage, while " **Rhett and Lin** k" collaborate with other creators For attract of new subscribers. Using the media social to connect with your audience and collaborating with other content creators, you can extend your

influence beyond of Youtube.

 THE hit on Youtube born to do not overnight. " **Mark Rober** " created videos carefully designed that have evolved over time to respond to changing needs of his audience. Create a plan to long term for your chain which takes into account trends, comments from the public and new opportunities.

Even content creators top performers continue to learn and improve. " **Lilly Singh** " has evolved over the years to reflect his own personal development and community needs.

Be open to new ideas, to comments and changes and adopt a continuous learning attitude.

Matthew (Micode): As content creator programming, **Micode** was able create engaging tutorials with concrete examples and clear explanations. This has created a loyal community of passionate about technology.

Game Theorists : thanks to detailed analyzes and interesting theories about games video, this channel managed to attract a passionate audience and curious.
Emma **ChamberlainEmma** Chamberlain was able to create a unique visual aesthetic for his vlogs and created a real connection with his generation.
Michelle Phan : Michelle Phan has revolutionized the industry

beauty online by sharing makeup
tutorials.

Its success paved the way for
many producers of beauty
content. By synthesizing what
these creators have learned, you
can create a sheet of road to your
success on Youtube.
 Remember that each course is
unique, but in adopting the bases
of passion, quality, dedication
and continuous learning, you
achieve your dream of becoming
A Creator Youtube To hit.

Finally, this book explores the secrets of YouTube's success using examples of creators of content who have learned these principles. Your journey as YouTube creator is a exciting adventure and constant evolution.

So use what you got learned here, perfect your skills and create content that inspires, informs and entertains your audience. The world of YouTube awaits you with possibilities
unlimited. Good DIY and good chance.

Chapter 8: Analyze and Fit your Strategy

The road to success on YouTube is full of challenges and obstacles, but overcoming them creates a career sustainable. In This chapter, we discuss the challenges currents faced content creators and provide examples content creators Who have succeeded To THE overcome.

You learn to manage criticism, manage stress and keep growing even when things get complicated.

 Each Creator Youtube must inevitably face reviews and comments negatives. The story of "PewDiePie" is an example of how it managed to sift through the reviews and to constitute a loyal fan base.
Learn to separate the constructive comments from trolls and detractors and use constructive criticism like an opportunity for you improve.

Succeeding on YouTube can be mentally and emotionally exhausting. " **Jenna Marbles** " has openly shared his experiences of stress and anxiety with his community.

He showed how much he is important to take care of mental health and to take the time to recharge their batteries. Learn to recognize the signs of stress and to implement self-management strategies for maintain a healthy balance.

The algorithm of Youtube And THE online trends change constantly.

The Fine Brothers chain Entertainment managed to stay relevant by adapting to changes and creating a content that responds to the evolution interests of his audience. Be ready to adapt your strategy to changes of platform and to the tastes of the public.

reach a plateau of channel growth or coping financial challenges may be intimidating. " **Grace Helbig** " has gone through periods of doubt and of stagnation, but it has continued to create content

authentic that reflects its
unique personality.

Find creative ways to overcome
financial challenges and to
maintain your passion for content
creation.

Casey Neistat : Despite the
financial difficulties and
personal, **Casey Neistat** has
persevered. His passion for
content creation helped him
overcome obstacles and to
grow in so much that Creator.
Liza Koshy: Liza Koshy
succeeded survive criticism and
celebrity pressures

remaining true to itself and continuing to create content keen.

Matthew **SantoroMatthew** Santoro overcame mental health issues in openly sharing his experiences with his community. His honesty has strengthened ties with its subscribers.

Tati Westbrook : Tati Westbrook managed to cope with criticism and controversy in concentrating on her love For there beauty and continuing to create quality content.

By learning from creators who have overcome challenges, you can develop a mindset durable and resilient as YouTube creator. do not forget that success does not come without failures, but your determination and your passion will help you overcome obstacles and progress.

Finally, this chapter emphasizes the importance of consistency and perseverance in your journey as a creator Youtube. In adopting a attitude positive face to reviews, taking care of your well-being mentally, adapting to change and overcoming financial challenges, you can continue on your way to hit.

 Always remember that every challenge you overcome brings you closer of your goals in so much that Creator.

Chapter 9: Monetization And Growth keep on going

As a YouTube creator, you influence millions of people in the world. With with this power comes responsibility to create ethical content, responsible and positive.

In this chapter, we explore ethics and responsibilities faced by the creators and provide examples specific of creators who have succeeded in to balance their creativity with their responsibilities to their audience and society.

Your content can shape the attitudes and perceptions of your audience. **NikkieTutorials** East an example of a designer who encourages positivity and self-acceptance through makeup videos. Creating a respectful environment and inclusive, you can inspire and positively influence your audience.

 Transparency and authenticity are essential to win the trust of your audience.

" **Jaclyn Hill"** spoke frankly from his personal experiences, including the challenges she has faced in the industry the beauty.

By being honest and open with your audience, you create a strong and authentic connection.

Avoid to create content harmful, offensive or sensational. " **Logan Paul** " did facing a backlash after having posted a controversial video.

Choose your topics and avoid arguments for better understand.

Your responsibility towards your audience goes beyond entertainment.
Ethical use and data transparency personal of audience are
important in partnerships of sponsorship.

" **Zoe Sugg** " (Zoella) is a creator who collaborates with marks and remains transparent for his audience. respect life privacy of your public and indicate clearly the partnerships of sponsorship to maintain the trust.

Brownlee Brands : **MKBHD** is known for its reliability in product technical reviews. Her transparency and its approach ethics helped him win the public trust.

Hannah Hart: Hannah Hart has used its platform to promote self-acceptance and positivity. His posts inspiring strengthen the social responsibility of creators.
John and Hank Green (Vlogbrothers): The **Green Brothers** have created a community of share of

knowledge and values positive. Their ethical approach has helped create a safe space for learning and participation.

Simply Nailogical : Cristine Rotenberg aka Simply Nailogical avoid sensationalism and favor humor and positivity in his nail art.

These guidelines for creators will help to successfully manage THE ethical issues and responsibility in so much that YouTube creator. Your platform can have an impact positive on the lives of your audience and on there Company In her together.

In adopting a approach ethics and assuming the responsibility for the impact of your content, you can create a online space governed by positive values.

Finally, this chapter focuses on the importance of ethics and responsibility as YouTube content producer. Your platform touches million people and your job is to create content respectful, positive and ethical.

By combining your creativity with your commitment to well-being of your audience, you can use your platform For inspire, educate And to have A positive impact.

Chapter 10 : Evolve in as Creator of Content

The journey as YouTube content producer is a constant adventure learning, of growth And of development. In the last chapter we discuss the importance of development continuous as the creator of content, as well as the creation of a lasting legacy thanks to the content.

Real examples of creators who have continued their success and
left a lasting impact will be explored so you can create a legacy as Creator Youtube.

The long-term success on YouTube requires the ability to innovate And of reinvent. "Shane

Dawson " is an example of creator who went from videos humorous to captivating documentaries.
Be ready to explore new formats, to experiment and respond to the interests changes in your audience.

your passion and your dedication to your content will contribute to your success. "
Markiplier " maintained a passion for video games and humor throughout career.

By staying connected to what you passionate, you can

conserve energy and
the authenticity that attracted
your original audience.

The lasting impact you leave in
so much that Creator of content
goes beyond impressions and
subscribers. " **Hank Green** "
(Vlogbrothers) created a space
online based on education and
positivity, leaving behind a legacy
that transcends its own career.

By identifying the values and
messages you want convey,
YOU can create A legacy that
will inspire future generations.

Succeed on Youtube can be difficult, but he East important of find a balance between your online career and your life personal.

" **Superwoman** " (Lilly Singh) has talked about his experiences exhaustion and exhaustion professional, emphasizing
the importance of self-care and time management.

Find of the means of maintain a balanced life while pursuing your passion
line.

Casey Neistat : Casey Neistat went from vlog videos daily to documentaries more in-depth while maintaining its unique style.

His commitment to authenticity helped him create a lasting legacy.

Lilly Singh : Lilly Singh is past of Youtube To there television while maintaining its style humorous and positive. He created a legacy as a pioneer and model for other designers.

Tyler Oakley : Tyler Oakley is went from humorous videos to conversations on topics important. His engagement towards education and awareness enabled him to leave a lasting impact.

NigaHiga : **Ryan Higa** maintained its popularity by reinventing itself and by experimenting with new formats All in remaining faithful To his unique style.

By inspiring these creators, you can create an inheritance as that YouTube creator in full boom. The heart of your success lies in your ability to to grow, to inspire and to have a positive impact on your audience and on the world around you.

Finally, this chapter focuses on the importance of developing and build a legacy as Creator Youtube. Your journey as content creator offers an opportunity to personal growth, connect with your audience and leave a lasting positive impact.

Keep learning, growing and create content that reflects your passion and your values, because It is Thus that YOU will leave a

brand indelible on Youtube And beyond.

conclusion

Congratulations on completing this book, which covers all aspects success on YouTube. Your journey as a creator of content is unique, but the basics here can prepare you to success.

From the identification of your passion for content creation quality, optimization of referral to interaction with your audience, you have learned the foundations for success platform. YOU can to build a successful career on YouTube learning from creators of successful content.

Your journey begin by
exploring your passion and finding your niche unique. Like " **Safiya Nygaard** " and " **MKBHD** ", find what you motivates and creates content that really inspires you.

Don't be afraid to innovate
and to experiment, because
Shane

Dawson And **NikkieTutorials** have evolved over time.
 SEO is an element important so that your content be found, as pointed out " **Graham Stephan"**.

By using keywords relevant and understanding the basics of **SEO** , you can increase the visibility of your videos.

Public engagement, as " **Philip DeFranco** " and " **Shroud** " have done so, is essential for build a community loyal. By responding to comments, using interactive features and creating space for a respectful conversation, you strengthen the bond between you and your subscribers.

Social media and the marketing cross, such that " **David Dobrik** " and " **Rhett and Link** ", can extend your reach beyond of Youtube.

Use social media to interact with your audience other manners and collaborate with others creators of content For attract of new subscribers.

Meet the challenges and keep on get inspired by examples such as " **Casey Neistat" and "Liza Koshy"**. Manage reviews, take care of your well-being mind and adapt to change For go of the front.

By creating ethical content and responsible, you can leave a lasting positive impact, such as did " **Hank Green** " and " **Simple Nailological"** . Be transparent, avoid harmful content and use your platform to inspire And educate.

Ultimately, your legacy as a YouTube creator depends on your ability to develop and maintain your passion, as did " **Casey Neistat" and "Markiplier** ". Create content that reflects your values and leaves a positive impact that goes beyond of the views And of the subscribers.

Your journey as YouTube creator is a exciting adventure and constant evolution. By combining passion, creativity, ethics and responsibility, you can create a lasting and inspiring career.

Every video you post has the possibility of touching lives, to share knowledge and to create lasting memories. So use whatever you learned here, perfect your skills and keep creating content that reflects your authenticity and your vision.

  THE world of Youtube YOU waiting with possibilities infinite. Good creation and good luck as a creator Youtube !